SENTINELS OF SOLITUD

ST. GEORGE REEF

west coast lighthouses

CAPE MEARES

YAQUINA HEAD

SENTINELS OF SOLITUDE
west coast lighthouses

PHOTOGRAPHY BY CHAD EHLERS / TEXT BY JIM GIBBS

EZ Nature Books
Post Office Box 4206
San Luis Obispo, CA 93403

POINT ARENA

International Standard Book Number 0-945092-06-7

© 1981 by Graphic Arts Center Publishing Company

Publisher 1989 Revised Edition – EZ Nature Books
P.O. Box 4206, San Luis Obispo, CA 93403

This book authorized and published under special arrangement with
Graphic Arts Center Publishing Company in Portland, Oregon.

Printing and binding – Jostens Printing and Publishing Division

Printed in the United States of America

To my Grandma—
One of the oldest sources of light
on the West Coast.

Chad Ehlers

INTRODUCTION

It is the last act. The curtain is falling. A century of history is seriously threatened. Built on sea-girt insular rocks, on remote headlands and busy bays, lighthouses are unique expressions of human creativity and triumphs of engineering. Time, however, refuses to stand still, and sentiment has lost ground to the practical nature of our time. The once cherished structures are vanishing. Only valiant efforts can preserve those that still remain.

Water covers more than two-thirds of our globe, and by night, darkness covers the waters. Ever since man first went down to the sea in ships he has sought guideposts to lead him to safe harbor. As long as a vessel and her crew remain at sea, chances of survival, even in storm-tossed waters and pea-soup fogs, are far greater than when approaching shore. Outcroppings, treacherous shifting shoals, and jagged reefs doom the unwary mariner in the shadow of night. When fog crawls in and gales howl, lookouts must be doubled in coastal sea-lanes, for it is here the majority of shipwrecks and collisions occur.

Lights along shore go back to antiquity. Beginning with those who lit open fires on tall headlands and ending with the dedicated lighthouse keepers of more recent decades, a humanitarian role was perpetuated.

Today, much of the personal touch is missing but the work of safeguarding the mariner continues with technological innovations unknown a century ago. Tending lights and fog signals has, for the most part, become automated; faithful keepers — wickies — have passed to their rewards but several of the graceful old towers with prismatic lenses continue to fight for survival in the nuclear age. Behind their flashing rays of light and droning foghorns is a story that longs to be told.

Sentinels of the sea have stood watch along America's shore for less than three centuries, a brief interlude compared to the entire history: the Pharos of Alexandria displayed a pillar of open fire from lofty heights as early as 280 B.C. Early Mediterranean lights included fiery eruptions from mountains like Etna, Stromboli, and Vesuvius. Fire beacons, common during the Roman Empire's maritime glory, faded during the Dark Ages. They flamed with renewed vigor during the Renaissance and in passing centuries became more sophisticated and plentiful.

The first lighthouse in America, the Boston Lighthouse, circa 1716, was paid by charging merchant ships a penny a ton for services rendered. Though open fires guided ships as far as the Mission at San Diego at the end of the 1700s, no United States government light marked the shores of the Pacific Coast until the 1850s. Yet in less than one hundred years a glorious chapter surfaces. Legions of stories, some dramatic, some romantic, some tragic, unfold around lighthouses starring Pacific shores. The stories center around the ships that pass in the night and the men and women who faithfully trimmed wicks, wound clockwork mechanisms, and tended boilers, compressors, and generators.

Many lighthouses are now relics — museums, historic attractions, restaurants. A number of proud old sentinels have lost the original jewels in their crowns, and in some cases the tower remains but the lantern-house has been removed in favor of an exposed aero-marine beacon. Manicured station lawns and meticulously trimmed shrubs have turned to weeds and brambles while keepers' dwellings sit abandoned with broken windows. Oil lamps have been relegated to history, as have the personnel of the old United States Lighthouse Service.

In 1939, the United States Coast Guard assumed authority for lighting our coastal shores. But this responsibility was not necessarily geared to the historic preservation of outdated lighthouses. Marine lighting has become functional: plastic lenses atop posts, platforms on steel legs, huge self-contained ocean buoys. Electronic miracles such as radar, radio beacons, and Loran send reliable signals in weather which blinded or muzzled the traditional lights and foghorns.

Yet, through it all, several pioneer lighthouses remain in a fair state of preservation, a credit to their master builders. Some still display their original prismatic lenses which reflect and refract light beams into a central source. Such old watchtowers breast the sea unmoved by the onslaught of boiling surf erupting on gnarled rock, taking the icy bath of clinging fogs and the slashing snap of gale force winds. When the architectural symmetry of a lighthouse mingles with light and shadow and the rugged beauties of the seacoast, the effect is spiritual.

Though modern mariners may cast their lot with innovative navigational aids, they still hold a heartfelt nostalgia for the traditional lighthouse welcoming them back from a long sea voyage. The language of the lighthouse has also evaporated. Few remember the days when lighting fixtures revolved in a bath of mercury or turned effortlessly on ball bearings, or of the clockwork drive activated by heavy weights that unwound downward through a hollow drop tube in the center of the tower and required frequent winding.

Initially, only the most important lighthouses had revolving beacons. In most secondary lighthouses, fixed lights were common. All lighting was produced from oil flames, often in five-wick burners which were fed with sperm whale, mineral, coal, olive, or coconut oil. A six-wick burner consumed about two-thirds of a gallon an hour or around 1,750 gallons a year. Imagine the elation when the incandescent oil vapor lamps were introduced, and finally electricity. Ironically, many of the French Fresnel lenses, designed to work best with an oil flame worked well with electric bulbs. Some have survived for over a century and are still rendering service. It is to Augustin Jean Fresnel, the famed French scientist who died in 1827, that we owe the introduction of the Lenticular System, dating from 1819. The large Fresnels of the first order, composed of more than one thousand prisms of polished glass, measure six feet in diameter and ten feet high.

Fog signals have taken a similar route. The old fog bells, gongs, cannons, and steam whistles were replaced by diaphones, diaphragm and siren signals, which in turn have taken a backseat to electronic radio innovations that beam out signals in all types of weather.

In October of 1852, Congress named a nine-member Lighthouse Board composed of military personnel, scientists and engineers to head an organization that built and operated virtually all the lighthouses in the United States, until the Coast Guard assumed responsibility in 1939.

Though basically relegated to another age, lighthouses are noble human achievements, symbols of mercy and attendant peril, familiar with the drama that colors canvases, fills books, intrigues photographers. Monuments that point heavenward, they are the glorious signposts and symbols of ocean travel.

POINT CONCEPTION

QUOTES—

Eternal granite hewn from the living isle
And dowelled with brute iron, rears a tower
That from its wet foundation to its crown
Of glittering glass, stands, in the sweep of winds,
Immovable, immortal, eminent.

Robert Louis Stevenson

GRAYS HARBOR (WESTPORT LIGHTHOUSE)

LIME KILN

POINT BONITA

This is his country's guardian,
The outmost sentry of peace.

Robert Louis Stevenson

POINT ARGUELLO

The rocky ledge runs far into the sea
And on its outer point, some miles away,
The lighthouse lifts its massive masonry.

Longfellow

POINT ARENA

NEW DUNGENESS

Not merely walls of brick and stone upon aprons of solid rock but something almost mystical, a symbol of unceasing endurance, of steadfast vigilance.

Chad Ehlers

GRAYS HARBOR (WESTPORT LIGHTHOUSE)

MARROWSTONE POINT

YERBA BUENA ISLAND

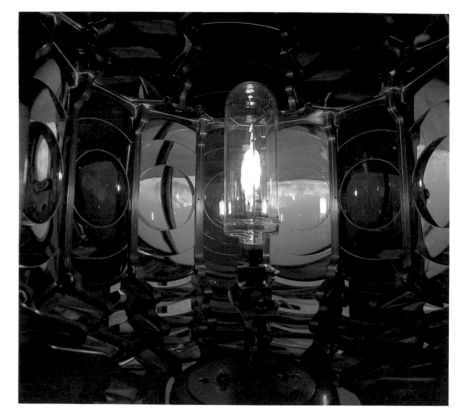

WEST POINT

ANACAPA ISLAND

Year after year, throughout the silent night,
Burns on for evermore that quenchless flame . . .

Longfellow

CRESCENT CITY

POINT PINOS

PATOS ISLAND

CATTLE POINT

LIME POINT

ALCATRAZ

YAQUINA HEAD

So to the night-wandering sailors, pale of fears,
Wide o'er the watery waste a light appears.
Which on the far seen mountains blazing high
Streams from some lonely watch-tower to the sky.

Homer

HECETA HEAD

POINT NO POINT

TILLAMOOK ROCK

POINT FERMIN

UMPQUA RIVER

COQUILLE RIVER (BANDON LIGHT)

HECETA HEAD

Lonely, bleak and worn, built to stand through time,
Stone and iron, lantern and siren,
Brick, rivet, and lime.

Jim Gibbs

OLD POINT LOMA LIGHT (CABRILLO NAT'L MONUMENT)

PIGEON POINT

EAST BROTHER ISLAND, SAN FRANCISCO BAY

LOS ANGELES

POINT LOMA LIGHT

TABLE BLUFF

POINT MONTARA

POINT VICENTE

CAPE FLATTERY (TATOOSH ISLAND)

ALKI POINT

ANACAPA ISLAND

WEST POINT

Still, broadcasting their beams and fog signals over the ocean,
beacons are outposts of civilization, solitary guardians
of the reefs and shoals that feed upon the unwary mariner's vessel.

Chad Ehlers

COQUILLE RIVER (BANDON LIGHT)

NORTH HEAD

POINT MONTARA

PIGEON POINT

ADMIRALTY HEAD

PIEDRAS BLANCAS

Perched on a craggy headland, commanding a shoal or rocky beach,
sentinels steadfastly guide mariners along their coastal highways.

Chad Ehlers

CAPE ARAGO

OLD POINT LOMA LIGHT (CABRILLO NAT'L MONUMENT)

CAPE BLANCO

POINT ROBINSON

POINT WILSON

POINT SUR

POINT VICENTE

POINT REYES

SAN LUIS OBISPO/PHOTO COURTESY U.S. COAST GUA[RD]

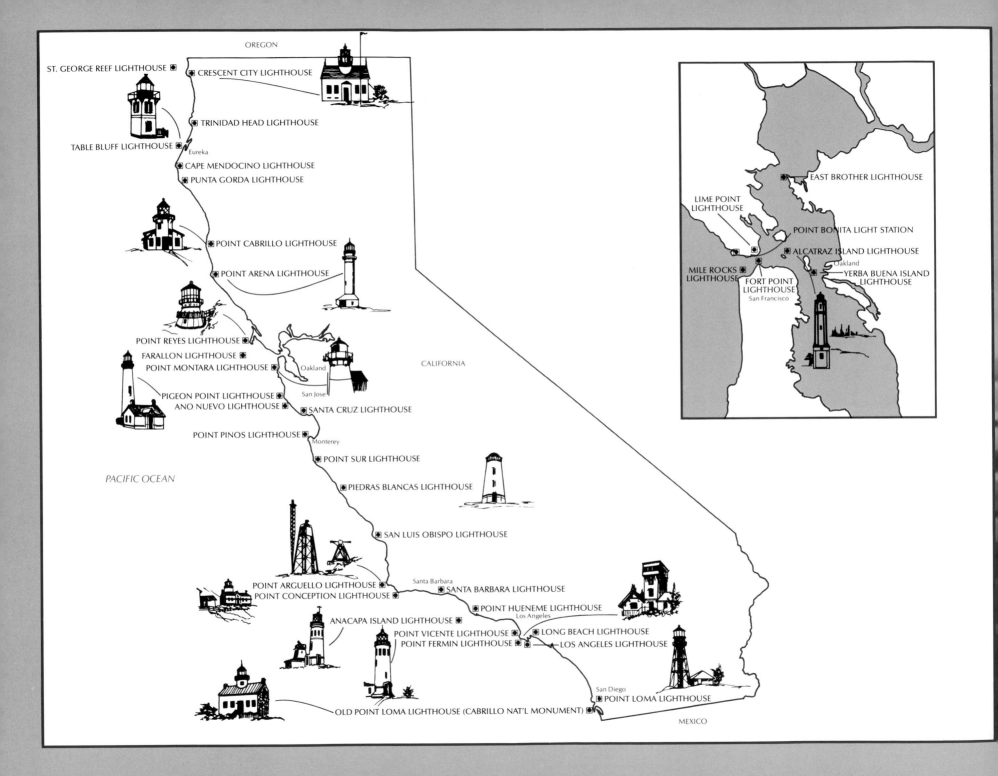

ST. GEORGE REEF LIGHTHOUSE ◙

OREGON

◙ CRESCENT CITY LIGHTHOUSE

◙ TRINIDAD HEAD LIGHTHOUSE

TABLE BLUFF LIGHTHOUSE ◙
Eureka

◙ CAPE MENDOCINO LIGHTHOUSE
◙ PUNTA GORDA LIGHTHOUSE

◙ POINT CABRILLO LIGHTHOUSE

◙ POINT ARENA LIGHTHOUSE

CALIFORNIA

POINT REYES LIGHTHOUSE ◙

FARALLON LIGHTHOUSE ◙
POINT MONTARA LIGHTHOUSE ◙
Oakland

PIGEON POINT LIGHTHOUSE ◙
ANO NUEVO LIGHTHOUSE ◙
San Jose

◙ SANTA CRUZ LIGHTHOUSE

POINT PINOS LIGHTHOUSE ◙
Monterey

◙ POINT SUR LIGHTHOUSE

PACIFIC OCEAN

◙ PIEDRAS BLANCAS LIGHTHOUSE

◙ SAN LUIS OBISPO LIGHTHOUSE

Santa Barbara

POINT ARGUELLO LIGHTHOUSE ◙
POINT CONCEPTION LIGHTHOUSE ◙
◙ SANTA BARBARA LIGHTHOUSE
◙ POINT HUENEME LIGHTHOUSE
Los Angeles

ANACAPA ISLAND LIGHTHOUSE ◙
POINT VICENTE LIGHTHOUSE ◙
◙ LONG BEACH LIGHTHOUSE
POINT FERMIN LIGHTHOUSE ◙ — LOS ANGELES LIGHTHOUSE

San Diego
◙ POINT LOMA LIGHTHOUSE

OLD POINT LOMA LIGHTHOUSE (CABRILLO NAT'L MONUMENT) ◙

MEXICO

◙ EAST BROTHER LIGHTHOUSE

LIME POINT LIGHTHOUSE

POINT BONITA LIGHT STATION

◙ ALCATRAZ ISLAND LIGHTHOUSE
Oakland

MILE ROCKS LIGHTHOUSE ◙
FORT POINT LIGHTHOUSE
YERBA BUENA ISLAND LIGHTHOUSE

San Francisco

Numbers in parenthesis indicate book pages where photographs
of respective lighthouses appear.

California

One of the oldest standing sentinels on America's Pacific shores, San Diego's **Old Point Loma Lighthouse** was constructed in the mid-nineteenth century atop a timeless monolith 462 feet above the sea. A site was cleared for the edifice in 1851, and finally, in August of 1854 the project got underway, using sandstone from Monterey and bricks from Ballast Point and Point Loma. Contractors Kelly and Gibbons, who had come west from Baltimore, hired W. J. McManus to supervise the work. Uncle Sam's bill was $30,000, which Congress authorized during the Millard Fillmore administration. The beacon began to shine in November of 1855.

But Point Loma's lofty perch spelled its demise when a cloud of complaints descended from navigators who said the beacon was often obscured by fog and low-hanging clouds. In 1891, the pioneer lighthouse was replaced by a new sentinel at a lower elevation. When rumor inaccurately suggested the abandoned structure was of Spanish origin, the lighthouse, after years of deterioration, was restored to crown the headland as part of the Cabrillo National Monument, which attracts more than two million visitors annually. Today it appears as it did in the mid 1800s when its oil lamp was first displayed. (39, 58)

In 1891, **Point Loma Lighthouse,** often called the grandson of the guardian atop the headland, was established. Eighty-eight feet above the sea at the west side of the entrance to San Diego Bay, the seventy-foot structure has little of the romantic qualities of its predecessor, but it guides ships far better. Some mariners claim its powerful beacon is visible twenty-three miles out to sea.

For several years, Point Loma Light had an active partner at nearby Ballast Point where Spanish explorer Cabrillo first landed in 1542. The latter station was erected in August, 1890, but after a half-century of service was replaced by a secondary light mounted on a piling. The passing parade of naval and merchant vessels and the countless number of smaller craft passing through the Silver Gate have long regarded Point Loma's friendly beacon as their official welcome to maritime San Diego, and there are no present plans to replace the lighthouse. (43)

Civic endeavor is responsible for restoring the old **Point Fermin Lighthouse** in greater Los Angeles as a living memorial to the past. Boasting Victorian gingerbread, the unique frame structure was built south of San Pedro in 1874. In 1945, it was replaced as an active lighthouse by a functional skeleton tower. In 1970, a light atop a pole replaced the skeleton.

Under the former Lighthouse Service, Point Fermin was for years a "favored" station, but not in the beginning. Coming west for a more healthy climate, Mary Smith, assisted by her sister, took the assignment as first keeper, but several months later they resigned their post because of loneliness.

The venerable old lighthouse is circled by Point Fermin Park, which encompasses a section of shore just before the Palos Verdes Peninsula cups San Pedro and Long Beach harbors. The shoreline, with its tidepools, marine fossils, and sea creatures is a pleasant interlude. (33, 36)

Long Beach Lighthouse was one of the first in the world to make a remarkable departure from long accepted, traditional lighthouse architecture. Located on the east end of the middle breakwater, it delights students of the modern. Established in 1949, labeled "the robot light," it was one of the first totally automated units: light, foghorn, and radio beacon all functioned within a rectangular tower set on a columnar base.

After the United States Coast Guard took over the Lighthouse Service in 1939, most of the civil service keepers retired. The few who remained schooled young recruits who assumed command, until one by one the facilities fell to automation. Radio technology also reduced the importance of the lighthouse as a primary navigational aid. Inaugurating an era of innovative ideas in navigation aids, Long Beach Lighthouse hastened the day "watched lights" became a thing of the past.

Los Angeles Lighthouse, a major safeguard of marine transportation since 1913, stands proudly at the outer end of the San Pedro breakwater, its green light bathing the watery acres nightly. Backdrop for many television and movie productions, the classic structure has long acted as potentate of busy Los Angeles Harbor.

Like the Tower of Pisa, the edifice leans slightly, victim of a furious gale several decades ago. But fear not, its designers and engineers allowed for such eventualities. Supported by strong pilasters, the heavily braced framework permits realignment whenever unequal settling occurs. Certainly, the aging sixty-nine-foot structure has felt its share of earthquake tremors.

And there have been several near misses by boats entering the harbor. Once a battleship scraped the jetty directly under its foundation. Fortunately the intruder careened back into its shipping lane, slightly the worse for the excursion. Angel Gate's ambassador remains a familiar landmark and sea beacon to millions of mariners the world over. (42)

Gracing the southwesterly end of the point, **Point Vicente Lighthouse** is a picturesque, sixty-seven-foot tower. Reached by a spur road off Palos Verdes Drive West, the sentinel has flashed its one million candlepower light since 1926.

Point Vicente laid claim to its own private ghost shortly after becoming operative. The wraith, a lady in a long, flowing gown, paraded after dark as the Fresnel lens threw its beams seaward. Old lighthouse personnel had no intention of thwarting the nightly activities of the phantom maiden, but a younger keeper decided to expose the apparition. He asserted the lady was merely an image caused by an unusual reflection when the lens revolved. His finding didn't sway the thinking of the senior keepers who firmly believed that every genuine lighthouse merits a ghost of one sort or another. To expose a wraith, they reasoned, was a risky business.

The rocky tentacles near the lighthouse have wrecked several ships. But its presence has prevented thousands of others from becoming ensnared. (46, 63)

Anacapa Island Lighthouse stands at the south side of Santa Barbara Channel's east entrance. Offering a commanding view 277 feet above the sea, the lighthouse is of modified Spanish architecture and was one of the last major sentinels constructed in America. Erected in 1932, the tower replaced a pyramidal skeleton structure established in 1912. Due to a rash of shipwrecks, agitation for a primary light goes back to 1868, but the cost of maintaining a manned light in such an isolated location stalled the effort.

Like her counterparts, Anacapa is now automated. Her island is part of the Channel Islands National Monument whose only residents are a few park rangers. Ironically, the lighthouse served as the backdrop for a television production about an old lightkeeper who was forced to retire.

Commercial fishermen frequent the waters surrounding Anacapa, and divers often search the elusive depths for the wreck of a Spanish galleon reputed to have sunk in the late 1700s with a fabulous cargo of gold, silver, and jewels. (21, 48)

Point Hueneme Lighthouse, a forty-eight-foot, square-shaped tower, rises from a one-story flat building. The light shines from the north side of Santa Barbara Channel's east entrance. Its low, sandy point is the toe of the Santa Clara Valley, fifty-three miles northwest of Point Fermin.

The government originally erected a fog signal in 1874 as an economy move due to the high cost of building a lighthouse on sea-girt Anacapa Island, eleven miles southwest. Though Anacapa received a beacon at a later date, the seamark at Point Hueneme remains essential to navigation, its fog signal warning ships hampered by fog from July through October.

The light is only fifty-two feet above sea level, and in the past, encroaching seas and erosion forced the removal of some station buildings.

The pioneer **Santa Barbara Lighthouse** was one of the eight original West Coast lighthouses. It was activated in December, 1856 after construction by George Nagle of San Francisco who made $8,000. Albert Johnson Williams was the first principal keeper, but nine years later, bored with his duties, he turned the lighthouse over to his wife. For forty years Julia Williams kept the station shipshape, faithfully trimming the wicks and polishing the brass and the glass prisms of the lighting apparatus. Additionally, she raised a family of three boys and two girls who became her assistants. A legend in her time, she was finally laid to rest at the age of eighty-one.

One mile east of Santa Barbara Point, in June, 1925 the lighthouse was jolted by a severe earthquake which demolished the structure. Keeper Weeks managed to rescue his mother, sister, and brother from the wreckage. In 1935, a mile east of Santa Barbara Point, a small, twenty-four-foot secondary light was erected 142 feet above water.

Point Conception Lighthouse stands as a monument to the eternal ambiguity of the sea. Sitting on a bold 200-foot headland, the fifty-two-foot tower sends flashing shafts of light above pounding breakers. On the north side of the west entrance to Santa Barbara Channel, awesome Point Conception has been called the Cape Horn of the Pacific because heavy northwest gales and meteorological changes resemble those at the bitter end of South America.

The original Point Conception lighthouse, established in 1856, was one of the Pacific's best and earliest ocean front navigational aids. But its location at the top of the headland was often obscured by fog, so in 1882 the station was rebuilt at a lower elevation. Here the light continues to shine, and a deep-throated fog signal blasts its warnings.

The ominous coast around Conception is little-changed from the virgin California of Richard Henry Dana, who in 1835 graphically described his ship clawing its way past the point in a howling gale. Dana also noted humped hills, killer whales, and a persistent fog back offshore.

So isolated and lonely was an early keeper of the light that he wrote the district inspector: "Point Conception lies sixty-five miles by land from the little village of Santa Barbara, the nearest point at which supplies can be obtained, the road to which place is only passable at very low water. The freight on goods amounts to more than my pay. How to convey my wood and water here I know not. That my situation here is truly distressing admits not to any doubt. My pay has not been forthcoming for four months." (9, 26)

Point Arguello Light glows on a narrow, jagged projection. Its offshore outcroppings are the graveyard of many ships and those who manned them. Mariners consider it one of the most dangerous areas along the entire coast, and a light, fog signal, and radio beacon an absolute necessity.

Despite constant agitation, it was 1901 before an official lighthouse marked the point. In 1934, that structure was replaced by another lighthouse, a rectangularly shaped forty-eight-foot tower. Now a pole light provides illumination.

Northward at the Honda, in the fall of 1923, seven United States Naval destroyers were torn open on the point's rocky manacles, while other squadron units narrowly escaped. Twenty-two blueclads lost their lives under a mantle of fog, and the survivors fought a desperate battle to gain the shore after escaping the wreckage.

Nearby, the sidewheel steamer *Yankee Blade* was wrecked in September, 1854. The ship allegedly carried $153,000 in gold bullion. A portion was never accounted for which brought cries of barratry. (15)

San Luis Obispo Lighthouse, built in 1890 on a bold headland, stands in seclusion awaiting its fate. Nearby, a functional navigation light shines from a pole structure at Point San Luis with fog signal and radio beacon nearby. The frame lighthouse, like many of its breed, has been "put out to pasture." Once faithfully attended, it requires tender care from historically minded volunteer civilians.

The first fog signal at the station was a ten-inch whistle which demanded a big head of steam in the boiler house before it could be sounded. It was later replaced by a two-tone diaphone horn.

The contrast between past and present is obvious along this part of the California coast. Here, the disposition of the old lighthouse remains complex: it stands on the outer grounds of the Diablo Canyon Atomic Power Plant, off limits to the general public. (65)

Graceful, tapering **Piedras Blancas Light** still lifts its massive masonry, but its iron lanternhouse was removed in favor of an exposed functional aero-marine beacon. Completed in 1875, the lighthouse maintained its lonely vigil on a wind-swept portion of the California coast for more than a century. The seventy-four-foot tower sits on a plant-covered knoll, and its sweeping beacon is seen eighteen miles at sea.

Today the grounds, occupied by the California State Fish and Wildlife Department, are closed to the public. But those who visited the area during periods of foggy weather have not forgotten the rasping, penetrating cry of the Piedras Blancas fog signal, loud enough to shatter eardrums. (57)

Twenty-five miles south of Monterey, **Point Sur Lighthouse** is the center of Big Sur country grandeur, a mecca for naturalists, photographers, painters, and writers. The land draws the kind of people that would just as soon have the world stand still and leave the place the way God made it.

The lighthouse is a gray stone tower atop a fog signal building. At first it appears perched on a low, turtle-backed island, but a sandy causeway connects it to the mainland. A road goes out to its base, but from there visitors don hiking shoes.

Built in 1889, the lighthouse gained a reputation for the 395 steps that led to its shelf. Easier access is now available. The focal plane of the light is 250 feet above the sea, and the great black butte on which it stands boasts an elevation of 362 feet. The station has a radio beacon, and a United States navy oceanographic research facility stands nearby. (63)

Point Pinos Lighthouse has a winning personality that attracts numerous visitors. Standing on a point at the south side of the entrance to Monterey Bay, it is typical of the architecture used in the earliest Pacific Coast lighthouses—the tower rises from the center of the lightkeeper's dwelling. In the middle of a golf course, the sentinel remains alive and well when most pioneer edifices have been decommissioned, razed, or left as fading monuments of another era: Point Pinos was converted into a Coast Guard museum featuring local maritime history.

Second only to the lighting of the original Alcatraz Island beacon, it was first illuminated in February 1855. Though suffering many earthquakes, none did as much damage as the 1906 convulsion. When the shaking stopped, the granite-faced lighthouse was so badly damaged it was overlaid with reinforced concrete.

For forty years Point Pinos light was under the all-seeing eyes of feminine attendants who took great pride in their work. Visitors have always received a cordial welcome. Fog is frequent, but gales are rare on Monterey Bay, and though several coastal vessels have met their waterloo on outcroppings off the point, the light, fog signal, and radio beacon have prevented countless tragedies. (24)

Santa Cruz Light beams from a white lanternhouse atop a red brick tower attached to a masonry building. A "memorial lighthouse" built in 1967, it is an impressive feature at the west side of the entrance to Santa Cruz Harbor.

The first lighthouse at Santa Cruz was a frame structure with a small square tower rising from the lightkeeper's dwelling which featured a red roof, white lantern housing and green blinds. The tower stood thirty-five feet high and displayed a fifth order light with a fixed red characteristic. Illuminated New Year's Day, 1870, the structure was moved to safer ground when undermined by three large sea caverns.

The first lightkeeper was itinerant New England preacher Adna A. Hecox. After he died in 1883, his daughter Laura became guardian of the light and for thirty-three years shared a proud tradition with her late father. (23)

A little islet known as **Ano Nuevo,** less than a mile off Point Ano Nuevo, is the quiet home of a forty-nine-foot pyramidal skeleton tower which serves as a day beacon only. Until 1948, Ano Nuevo showed a navigation light by night, but due to changing marine traffic patterns, a whistle buoy took its place.

Located eighteen miles northwest of Point Santa Cruz, Ano Nuevo was marked by a fog signal and lens-lantern ten years before the turn of the century. In a severe earthquake on October 22, 1926, the station's lighting apparatus was shaken out of its base and fell through the hatch, smashing to pieces on the watch room floor. A standby lantern was installed, but a second jolt destroyed it also. Two additional quakes further damaged the tower and nearby buildings, but the wickies improvised and soon had a light shining seaward once again.

Point Ano Nuevo State Reserve protects sea birds and sea mammals. Frequently the rim of the islet is alive with hundreds of barking sea lions and screeching birds basking on the rocky shelves.

Pigeon Point Lighthouse is one of the truly magnificent sentinels on the California coast. Looming majestically skyward from a shelf of rock, it attains a height of 115 feet, sharing honors as the tallest outer guardian on the Pacific Coast with the tower at Point Arena.

Countless travelers on Coast Highway 1 have thrilled at the sight of the lighthouse which for the most part has remained unaltered since completion in 1872, when the Fresnel lens, lighting apparatus, and clockwork mechanism first became operative. The original lens is not in use; the Coast Guard has mounted an aero-marine type beacon on the tower gallery.

The conical-shaped masonry structure remains well preserved despite years of service. Though it stands where the British ship *Sir John Franklin* was wrecked shortly before the advent of a beacon, the point is named for an earlier shipwreck. The *Franklin* ran afoul of the rocks in January 1865 and the captain and twelve crewmen perished. The American clipper *Carrier Pigeon* was lost on a stormy June night in 1853, a little north and five hundred feet offshore. Her master, Captain Azariah Doane, and his crew survived. Today, the Coast Guard maintains a radio beacon antenna near the lighthouse. (Cover, 14, 40, 54, 55)

Point Montara Lighthouse was a fog signal station from 1875 until 1900 when a light was installed to better mark the searoad to San Francisco Bay. Located just off the highway near Pacifica, since 1928 Point Montara's soldier-like, thirty-foot, conical tower has stood seventy feet above the sea.

Point Montara is the seaward end of a Montara Mountain spur. With cliffs sixty feet high, flanked on its shoreline by outcroppings waiting to snag the unwary vessel, it is a dangerous locale in thick weather. Mariners must use extreme caution inside the thirty-fathom curve.

The steamer *Colorado* was stranded on an offshore ledge in November, 1868, the ship *Acuelo* was gutted below Point Montara in November, 1872 with the loss of her $150,000 coal, iron, and grain cargo. Such tragedies spurred the fog signal's installation.

In July, 1980, the Point Montara lighthouse grounds were the first to be leased by the American Youth Hostels Inc. as part of a growing system of recreational facilities. Cooperating in the effort were the California State Parks System and the Twelfth Coast Guard District. (45, 52)

Named Los Farallones by early Spanish mariners, the rocky, barren islets are scattered in a broken line for about seven miles like a set of rotten, snagged teeth. Set in these devouring jaws, **Farallon Lighthouse** has a history that could fill a book.

The Gold Rush of 1849 demanded a lighthouse to protect an endless parade of ships. In 1852, the loftiest of the isles, Southeast Farallon, twenty-three miles west of San Francisco, was chosen as the most logical site, but it was with extreme difficulty that a forty-one-foot masonry edifice was erected on the rock-bound crown 317 feet above sea level. Back-breaking effort was necessary, and without the use of mules the work might never have been completed, for all materials had to be hauled up the precipitous cliffs where rock slides were common.

When the French ship *St. Joseph* arrived at San Francisco in December, 1854 with wine for the city and lens and lighting apparatus for the Farallon, it was discovered the tower was too small to handle the big glass fixture. The builders had to tear down all the masonry and start over again. The light was finally displayed in January, 1856.

The same structure continues in use today with a modern light, fog signal, and radio beacon on a twenty-four-hour automated status since the winter of 1972 when the last keeper, Brent Franze, was removed by the Coast Guard. The light's nearby companion, the San Francisco Lightship (1898-1971) was replaced by a large ocean buoy.

History colors the Farallons. On July 24, 1579 Sir Francis Drake drew upon "the great store of seals and birds" there to replenish supplies. And in 1819-20 Russians and Aleuts established a base to gain salted sea lion meat for the Czar's Fort Ross settlement. (87)

When completed in 1906, the year of the San Francisco earthquake, **Mile Rocks Lighthouse** was one of the most unusual sentinels in the nation. For a half mile off San Francisco's Point Lobos, a series of dangerous, mostly submerged rocks extend into the Golden Gate. The outermost, a pair of twenty-foot high, grim, grotesque obstructions stand about one hundred feet apart. The outer and slightly larger rock was chosen as the site, and under the most difficult of conditions the lighthouse was erected. Its base occupies virtually the entire diameter of the wave-swept barrier where currents are swift and treacherous, and the finished project was nothing less than an engineering triumph. All materials were hoisted up from the sea by derrick.

It was the tragic loss of the steamship *City of Rio de Janeiro* in February, 1901 that prompted funds for a lighthouse. The liner struck nearby Fort Point Ledge while entering the Gate in a thick fog. One of the greatest sea tragedies in California history, she went down with 129 persons.

Many labeled Mile Rocks "Devils Island" because of the lonely vigil and the difficulty of maintaining the station, but through the years its presence has proved invaluable to marine traffic. With automation, an unfortunate dismantling operation was begun in 1965. Three tiers of the lighthouse were removed, and a submarine cable extended from Point Bonita. A new reflecting light and fog signal were installed on the lower tier, along with a helicopter pad. The job was finished in the summer of 1966 at a cost of $110,000, and many San Franciscans lamented the extreme surgery on their beloved tower.

Fort Point Lighthouse marks San Francisco Bay's most formidable bastion, old Fort Winfield Scott. Though no light has shone from the tower since construction of the Golden Gate Bridge, the National Park Service preserved and restored the lighthouse. Last keeper, George Cobb, resigned his post in 1934. Keeper James Rankin, who was assigned duty in 1878, gave forty-one years of service and was credited with saving the lives of several distressed persons.

In 1852, the first lighthouse, a Cape Cod-type dwelling surrounding a tower, was constructed. But when the U.S. Army elected to fortify the entrance to San

Francisco Bay, the three-month-old unused building was torn down to make room for a gun emplacement. In its place, between the fort and the seashore, a second sentinel, a thirty-six-foot truncated, frame edifice was erected and lighted in March of 1855. When erosion threatened the ground on which this second lighthouse stood, it too was removed. The third and remaining structure, dating from 1864, is an iron, twenty-seven-foot skeleton tower surmounted by a closed watch room and lanternhouse. For many years lightkeepers and their families lived side by side with military personnel. Protruding from the top of the fortress walls like a turret, the tower looms eighty-three feet above fortress grounds.

Like many of the early lighthouses, the lens at Fort Point consisted of three panels enhanced by parabolic reflectors. The lighting fixture revolved on twenty-four ball bearings, and the clockwork drive, activated by a seventy-pound weight, unwound downward through a twenty-foot drop tube. Every four hours, the keepers wound the clockwork. (88)

Established in 1883 as a fog signal station, **Lime Point Lighthouse's** dual, twelve-inch steam whistles warned shipping whenever fog drifted through the Golden Gate. Some years 150,000 pounds of coal were required to feed the boilers.

A lens-lantern was eventually attached to the fog signal house and first lighted in November, 1900 along with similar fixtures at Point Montara and Angel Island fog stations. The station weathered the 1906 earthquake with only minor damage, and in 1937, though totally dwarfed by the 740-foot-high Golden Gate Bridge, continued to provide essential service.

Initially, rock slides crashed down from the cliffs. The building of the bridge solved that problem but substituted another: Coast Guard attendants found themselves dodging bottles flung from the span by thoughtless travelers.

In June of 1960, under the shadow of the towering bridge, the freighter *India Bear* crashed into the base of the facility and inflicted $7,500 in damages before limping off to a nearby shipyard. The ship's repairs totaled $60,000. Now the lighthouse is floodlit at night. (28)

Alcatraz Island Lighthouse, in San Francisco Bay, shared the first portion of its existence with an infamous prison. Deactivated, the prison has become a popular tourist attraction, and the lighthouse still sends shafts of light over bay area waters. In 1909, the eighty-four foot, reinforced concrete tower, one of the highest in the state, replaced the original lighthouse, which was the first to display a light on the entire Pacific Coast.

That pioneer sentinel was a Cape Code-style edifice surrounding a short tower, an economical one-family design passed by the U.S. Lighthouse Board set up in the early 1850s to modernize the nation's marine lighting system. Maryland contractors Gibbons and Kelly were awarded a contract by the U.S. Secretary of the Treasury to construct seven lighthouses in California and one at Columbia River's Cape Disappointment. Of the eight, Alcatraz was the first completed. In June of 1854, after shipment from France, a fixed white light of the third order was displayed, marking a milestone in marine history. Several months later, the constant fog demanded erection of a fogbell.

In 1970, after the prison closed, a band of Indians claiming grandfather rights invaded the isle. Chaos followed, including a fire that considerably damaged the lower portion of the lighthouse. Eventually, federal agents landed and removed the few hungry squatters still remaining. (29)

East Brother Lighthouse, established in March 1874 on a small islet off the Contra Costa shore, was typical of early San Francisco Bay family lighthouses. Victorian in design, with a frame construction, it was beautifully maintained and is one of the few of its breed still active. Originally the old fog bell was rung by hand when boilers, for lack of water, were unable to produce sufficient steam. Later a cistern was installed. In 1934, the station was ordered closed, but navigators and shipowners protested vehemently and within a few days the order was lifted. Again in 1968 the Coast Guard announced closure of the station in favor of an exposed automated beacon. But those who had a "love affair" with the ornate old structure had it placed on the National Register of Historic Places. And today its light still shines, serviced by Coast Guard personnel. (41)

Lighting San Francisco Bay waters since October, 1875, **Yerba Buena Island Lighthouse** was at first something of a welfare case. Its fifth order lighting apparatus was borrowed from the abandoned Yaquina Bay Lighthouse in Oregon, the fog bell was brought in from the old Point Conception station. The attractive little Victorian-style frame tower and the station outbuildings fit so well into its isle's terra firma it seemed they always had been there.

Originally, masses of goats roamed Yerba Buena Island. Eventually, ferryboat travelers grew familiar with the station. First used by the military, the island suffered water shortages and communication lapses. Children of lightkeepers were either educated by their parents or sailed via station boats to the mainland when weather and sea conditions permitted. The Twelfth Lighthouse District established a depot on the isle as early as 1873 to service navigation aids and surface craft, and to this day the Coast Guard operates a repair depot.

Yerba Buena gained prominence when the San Francisco Bay-Oakland Bridge opened in 1936, for the islet was tunneled through as a mid-bay bridge support. Today, the Twelfth Coast Guard District's commanding officer and family make their home in the station's original dwelling, and the grounds are kept in the apple pie order of former years. (20)

Point Bonita Light Station on the north side of the entrance to the Golden Gate was the last of California's fifty-nine to undergo automation. In late 1980, Chief Boatswain Mate John Dusch, officer in charge, made the final entry in the station log. Automation marked the end of an era: the first principal keeper assigned to Point Bonita fired up the lantern in the original lighthouse in April, 1855. As an early guardian of the light once wrote his district inspector: "There are no inhabitants within five miles from this point, from San Francisco to Point Bonita; there is no direct communication but by chance...."

In 1856, the coast's first fog signal was placed at Point Bonita. With more than one thousand hours of fog annually, the cannon had to be fired at frequent intervals day and night. The firing became a major staff complaint; in the late 1850s, seven different keepers resigned their posts in protest.

The original Bonita light was replaced by the present masonry structure in 1877, and a new fog signal house was added in 1902. Today, the 60,000 candlepower light and fog signal are monitored by computers. Crumbling rock has long posed a problem. To reach the lighthouse one must traverse a narrow footbridge, which is hazardous walking in high winds. (12, 13)

Old **Point Reyes Lighthouse** stands where fog persists, and one hundred-mile-an-hour winds follow on the heels of driving rain. The station was placed under the auspices of the National Parks Service as a historical site. The Coast Guard has placed a functional light, elevated above a small building and a cooperating fog signal, at the western pitch of the point, 265 feet above the sea where the peninsula flirts with the San Andreas Fault.

For more than a century, from December 1870 until 1975, the lighthouse had personnel attending to the first order lens which was composed of more than a thousand prisms of polished glass. By night the light flashed its warning from an elevation of 294 feet. Three hundred stairs leading down to the veteran structure still remain. Ascending those stairs in adverse weather and high winds present an adventure which, once undertaken, is never forgotten.

In bygone years, problems plagued the station. The fog signal house burned down in 1872; boilers for the new replacement consumed a remarkable 140 pounds of coal per hour; two of the keepers drowned within two years. More recently, the typhon foghorn, blasting continuously for eight days and nights, paled the faces of attendants.

Situated eighteen miles north of Farallon Light, at the end of Sir Francis Drake Boulevard, the old Reyes sentinel has become a focal point of the Point Reyes community and the Point Reyes National Seashore. Around the great headland, where up to twenty-seven hundred hours of fog have been recorded yearly, numerous shipwrecks have occurred. Heading the list is the Spanish galleon *San Augustin,* which crashed ashore in 1595 with an exotic cargo from the Indies. (64)

On a spur road west of Highway 1, near the town of Point Arena, glimmers **Point Arena Lighthouse,** a giant index finger pointing heavenward. Toward the end of a narrow strip of dramatic seacoast, the sentinel rises 115 feet, sharing honors with Pigeon Point Lighthouse as the coast's tallest.

The pioneer structure was commissioned in May 1870 and held its vigil on the windswept point until the frightening 1906 earthquake demolished the station. The lighting apparatus was saved and placed in a temporary tower until the new tower was lighted in January 1908. One of the nation's first reinforced concrete stations, its designer and engineer claimed it earthquake-proof.

Just after Pearl Harbor, Point Arena's legendary keeper, Bill Owens, reported to authorities that he and his wife had sighted a Japanese submarine off the point. Naval officials took the report with a grain of salt until a few days later the tanker *Emidio* was torpedoed off Cape Mendocino. In 1949, the British cargo ship *Pacific Enterprise* was wrecked near the lighthouse, her master, homebound on his final voyage after forty years of seafaring without mishap. In 1977, the station was automated and left to its solitude. (6, 16)

Point Cabrillo Lighthouse graces the coast a mile west of Highway 1 near the colorful town of Mendocino. Amid a pastoral setting, the lighthouse appears to be a white-painted country church. One imagines the strains of *Let the Lower Lights Be Burning* rising from within.

On closer examination, however, one views with fascination the stalwart sentry of another era. Though the big Fresnel lens is still housed in the lantern above the frame tower, automation in the early 1970s saw a large functional reflecting beacon mounted on the structure's roof.

The lighthouse was commissioned in June 1909 and soon became a constant companion to a grand fleet of steam schooners plying the redwood trade, darting in and out of dogholes along the coast. The fearless Scandinavian skippers who manned them blasted their whistles when passing.

A frequent visitor is octogenarian William Owens, who served eleven of his thirty-three working years as the keeper of the Cabrillo light. Asked about automation, Owens remarked, "Anything automatic always goes haywire just when you need it. We'll have a big wreck one of these days." (60)

Punta Gorda Lighthouse rests in lonely abandon along a little-visited section of the northern California coast. Between Shelter Cove and Cape Mendocino the wild, ragged coastline remains almost as pristine as it was ten thousand years ago.

When the coastal liner *Columbia* went to her grave sixteen miles south of Punta Gorda in 1907 with the loss of eighty-seven lives, a great cry for more aids to navigation arose. So, the lighthouse station, including spacious family dwellings, was built below the massive rolling hills. Great difficulty was experienced in transporting building materials from distant Petrolia, and it was not until January, 1912 that the isolated station began full operation. Always a costly station to maintain, the Coast Guard abandoned it in the winter of 1951 and placed a lighted whistle buoy offshore to compensate for the blacked-out lighthouse. Under the Bureau of Land Management all the station buildings except the lighthouse were purposely burned down in 1970. The sentinel stands alone with an empty lantern.

On the beach near the structure lie the bones of two shipwrecks of early days—the steamers *St. Paul* and *Humboldt.* Close by lies the wreckage of the whistle buoy which was torn from its moorings in heavy seas.

Cape Mendocino Lighthouse is another regal sentinel relegated to retirement. In its place a functional light shines seaward from a polelike structure 515 feet up the west slope of the cape and seventy yards from the old lighthouse.

Cape Mendocino, 185 miles north of San Francisco, is a precipitous headland, but it was the desired landfall of Spanish navigators returning from the Orient en route to Mexico. Sugar Loaf, 326 feet high, lying just to the west, is connected with the mainland only at low tide.

Resting in secluded majesty, the old lighthouse was one of the country's highest. From its perch 422 feet above the shoreline, the forty-three-foot iron-plated structure long marked the important Pacific turning point.

Prompting completion of the lighthouse in December, 1868 was the crash of the liner *Northerner* with the loss of thirty-eight lives. Materials and supplies for the project were landed by running the ocean surf, a highly dangerous operation. In 1881, a visiting lighthouse inspector was drowned trying to make a landing in an open boat. Numerous earthquakes have rocked the station, inflicting damage to outbuildings, but seldom to the lighthouse.

Table Bluff Lighthouse is gradually fading away. Only the forsaken tower remains. Abandoned by the Coast Guard, its future is questionable as it perches atop a 165-foot bluff with a commanding view of the Pacific and Humboldt Bay. The tower stands next to Lighthouse Ranch, a religious community which has taken over most of the old lighthouse reservation. Uncle Sam automated the lighthouse in 1953 and dropped it as an aid to navigation in 1972. Both the nearby towns of Lolita and Eureka have expressed interest in the tower, but at this writing no preservation work has been done.

The lighthouse, activated in October, 1892, replaced veteran Humboldt Harbor Lighthouse. The older structure, dating from 1856, gradually eroded away under encroaching seas because its foundation was on sand. The initial keeper of the new facility, Tony Schmoll, blinked his light back and forth with Blunts Reef's offshore lightship. In 1921, the liner *Alaska* went down off the reef with heavy loss of life. (44)

Trinidad Head Lighthouse is one of the biggest little lighthouses on the coast. The masonry tower, only twenty-five feet high, sticks out like a thumb on the slope of its massive headland. At an elevation of 196 feet, the little tower affords a spectacular view of the Pacific. The lighthouse has seen continuous activity since December, 1871 when principal keeper Jeremiah Kiler arrived.

Located near the busy little fishing port of Trinidad, the lighthouse has one mark of distinction claimed by no other. In December, 1914, in the words of keeper F. L. Harrington, writing in the station log: "The sea increased and at 3:00 P.M., on December 31, waves washed a number of times over Pilot Rock, 103 feet high, a half mile south of the head." A half hour later, after Harrington had set the lens in motion, his account reads: "It struck the bluff with solid impact, drove up the cliff and sent green water splashing over the 196-foot mark, bathing the entire area around the lighthouse. The lens stopped revolving and the land shook." The Trinidad wave was one of the most gigantic ever recorded.

The lighthouse served maritime traffic with its old oil light until 1942 when it was electrified. In 1948, the town of Trinidad created a park and built a cement replica of the old lighthouse as a tourist attraction. Mounting the station's old lens inside, they placed the original four thousand-pound fog bell nearby. (53)

Crescent City Lighthouse, long inactive as an aid to navigation, has become the area's major maritime attraction. Preserved near its original state, the grand old structure nestles compactly atop a little island directly off Battery Point. Only at low tide can one reach the mainland.

Congress appropriated $15,000 for the lighthouse in 1854, and in December, 1856 the light was first displayed. The assigned keeper, Theophilis Magruder, showed up Christmas Day and resigned his post three years later when an austerity program cut his yearly salary from $1,000 to $600.

The lighthouse dwelling is made of huge stone blocks. The tower which rises through its roof is of masonry construction. Despite decades of punishment, the sentinel remains a stalwart credit to its builders.

In 1953, the station was automated and later dropped from service altogether. In March, 1964, an Alaska earthquake triggered severe seismic tidal waves that swept the islet and destroyed a large section of the Crescent City waterfront but not the lighthouse. The Coast Guard has turned the old sentinel over to the Del Norte County Historical Society which maintains it as a maritime museum and tourist attraction. (22)

The deposed king of all Pacific Coast lighthouses is **St. George Reef Lighthouse.** It seems inconceivable, but the costliest aid to navigation ever constructed in modern times stands isolated and void of human life. In May, 1975 the colors were lowered, the door chained and padlocked. The old station derrick swung Chief Sebastian and Petty Officer Salter in the Billy Pugh net down to the deck of the Coast Guard cutter *Cape Carter*. The tower was left intact, with all its furnishings and equipment, even the lens and lighting apparatus. Due to its total exposure to the elements and the dangerous seas that have frequently engulfed the tower, the cost of maintenance and supply negates further use.

On a clear day the lighthouse, rising out of the sea like a giant monster, is visible six miles offshore. One of the best landside viewing spots is on Highway 101, near the Oregon – California border. Built on a perilous sea-washed rock, the virtually indestructible tower was completed in October, 1892 after nearly a decade of construction work. Faced with 1,339 huge interlocked granite blocks atop a solid core base, its total cost was $704,633, equal today to several million dollars. Its half-inundated rock stands near the wreck of the steamer *Brother Jonathan* which, in July, 1865, carried 166 persons to a watery grave.

While a station boat was lowered in a sling from the derrick in April, 1951, tragedy struck. An unexpected wave caught the craft, capsized it, and threw five Coast Guardsmen into the sea. Three perished. Seas as high as 160 feet have bathed the tower during roaring gales. Since closure of the light, a lighted horn buoy a mile west of Northwest Seal Rock warns shipping. (1)

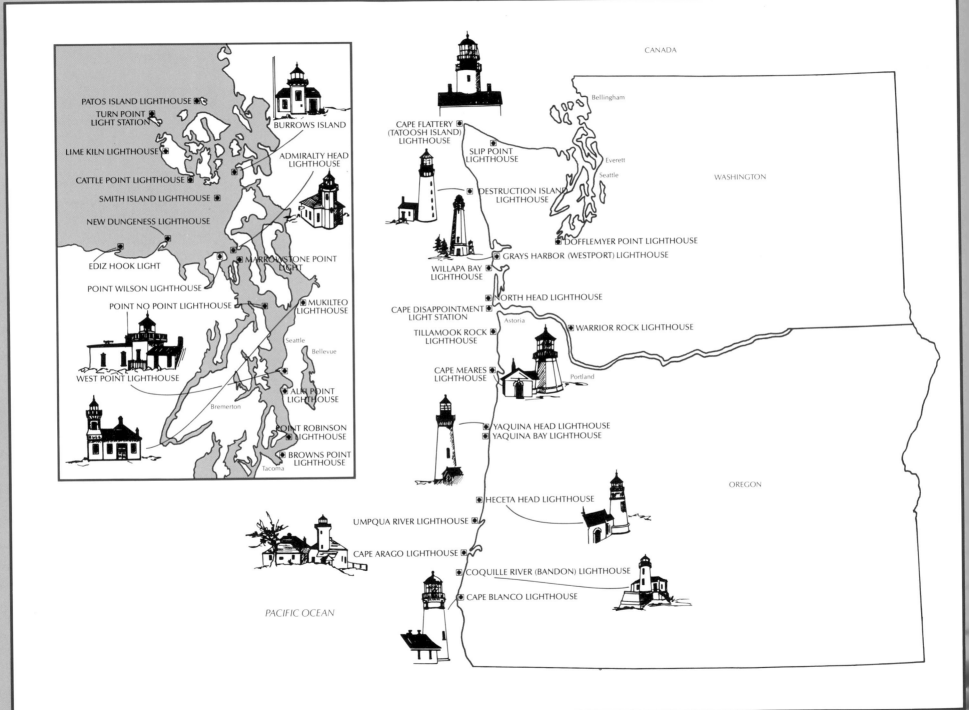

CANADA

Bellingham

PATOS ISLAND LIGHTHOUSE
TURN POINT
LIGHT STATION
LIME KILN LIGHTHOUSE
CATTLE POINT LIGHTHOUSE
SMITH ISLAND LIGHTHOUSE
NEW DUNGENESS LIGHTHOUSE
EDIZ HOOK LIGHT
POINT WILSON LIGHTHOUSE
POINT NO POINT LIGHTHOUSE
WEST POINT LIGHTHOUSE

BURROWS ISLAND

ADMIRALTY HEAD
LIGHTHOUSE

MARROWSTONE POINT
LIGHT

MUKILTEO
LIGHTHOUSE

Seattle

Bellevue

ALKI POINT
LIGHTHOUSE

Bremerton

POINT ROBINSON
LIGHTHOUSE

BROWNS POINT
LIGHTHOUSE

Tacoma

Everett

Seattle

WASHINGTON

CAPE FLATTERY
(TATOOSH ISLAND)
LIGHTHOUSE

SLIP POINT
LIGHTHOUSE

DESTRUCTION ISLAND
LIGHTHOUSE

DOFFLEMYER POINT LIGHTHOUSE

GRAYS HARBOR (WESTPORT) LIGHTHOUSE

WILLAPA BAY
LIGHTHOUSE

NORTH HEAD LIGHTHOUSE

CAPE DISAPPOINTMENT
LIGHT STATION

Astoria

WARRIOR ROCK LIGHTHOUSE

TILLAMOOK ROCK
LIGHTHOUSE

CAPE MEARES
LIGHTHOUSE

Portland

YAQUINA HEAD LIGHTHOUSE
YAQUINA BAY LIGHTHOUSE

OREGON

HECETA HEAD LIGHTHOUSE

UMPQUA RIVER LIGHTHOUSE

CAPE ARAGO LIGHTHOUSE

COQUILLE RIVER (BANDON) LIGHTHOUSE

CAPE BLANCO LIGHTHOUSE

PACIFIC OCEAN

Oregon

Oregon's most southerly major sentinel is **Cape Blanco Lighthouse.** The fifty-nine-foot, conical-shaped masonry tower was commissioned in December, 1870. Construction materials, including the $20,000 first order lens, carriage and lighting apparatus, had to be landed by boat and hauled up to the cape's summit. The original lens is still in service.

Beginning in 1875, keeper James Langlois saw service forty-two years, never stepping foot in any other lighthouse. For part of that time, two women acted as his assistants, Mrs. Bretherton and Mrs. Alexander. Mrs. Bretherton's appointment, official in 1903, gave her a salary of $550 annually. She was probably Oregon's first official female lighthouse keeper. Later, due to an austerity program or to sexual discrimination, the women lost their jobs.

The beach near the mouth of the Elk River, where poet Joaquin Miller courted Minnie Myrtle, gives a striking view of the lighthouse and its breathtaking setting. Despite the primitive access, the lighthouse log recorded that, over a very rough washboard road, wagons and buggies brought 4,042 visitors in the decades between 1896 and 1916. Today, the station, Oregon's highest and most westerly, is reached by a narrow six-mile road west of Highway 101. (61)

Coquille River (Bandon) Lighthouse was restored in recent years as a state historic attraction. Abandoned by the Coast Guard in 1939, deteriorating, for several years its fate was in doubt. Standing abreast Coquille Bar's north jetty, the unique masonry tower, attached to a former fog signal building, entered service in 1896 at a cost of $17,600.

The sentinel rendered double duty as a seacoast beacon and harbor entrance light during coastal shipping's "Golden Age." Considered by navigators and pilots the most dangerous bar in Oregon, at the turn of the century the Coquille swept a three-masted sailing schooner into the base of the lighthouse. Unlike most vessels that locked horns with the bar, the windjammer sailed again. (37, 51)

Cape Arago Lighthouse shines seaward from a forty-four-foot tower, one hundred feet above the sea. Located south of Coos Bay and North Bend—the softwood capital of the world—the sentinel's name is somewhat misleading, for it is not located at Cape Arago but two and a half miles north. The lighthouse sits on a rocky, partially wooded islet close inshore and is reached by a foot bridge.

Built of reinforced concrete, the octagonal tower and fog signal building form a single unit which replaced the 1909 frame structure. The site's first lighthouse, commissioned in November, 1866, when Cape Arago was named Cape Gregory, was a wrought iron sentinel at the islet's seaward end. Erosion demanded a replacement within fifty years. Many ships were wrecked along the shores of Coos County, and for years the lighthouse was accompanied by a lifesaving station maintained in the lee of the islet to aid distressed seamen. Today a fog signal and radio beacon are used, and the light remains a vital factor in navigation. Nearby, two favorite state parks—Cape Arago and Shore Acres—attract thousands of vacationers. (56)

Umpqua River Lighthouse, an elegant sixty-five-foot masonry tower has graced the delightful Umpqua shores since 1894. Situated just off Highway 101 south of Reedsport, it is a prime tourist attraction, focal point of the Umpqua Lighthouse State Park. Surrounded by tall evergreens and acres of sand, the beacon has long stood a symbol of safety for vessels approaching Umpqua River's treacherous bar. Within the dome of the tower the first order Fresnel still reflects and refracts light in rainbow brilliance.

The Umpqua River Lighthouse, erected near the river entrance in 1857, was Oregon's first coastal beacon. But river freshets and ocean breakers undermined the pioneer structure, and in February, 1861, it collapsed.

Despite constant pleas, more than three decades passed before Uncle Sam favored that primitive sector of maritime Oregon. In the interim, several vessels were wrecked on the river bar and numerous lives were lost. Today the lighthouse guides the commercial fishboats, tugboats, and lumber barges frequenting Winchester Bay and upriver portals. (37)

In all the world there may be no more spectacular setting for a seacoast beacon than the **Heceta Head Lighthouse** throne from which millions have viewed unending beauty. All northbound travelers on Coast Highway 101 see the lighthouse. Numerous visitors have walked the evergreen-lined paths or the beaches below to paint, photograph, or cogitate. Just south are the famous Sea Lion Caves which offer another grand vista.

Built at a cost of $180,000, completed in 1894, the masonry structure is overlaid with cement plaster. Building materials were delivered to Florence via the Siuslaw River, then barged to a cove below the lighthouse. In those years, there was no coast road. The mammoth first order lens, carriage, and lighting apparatus, contrary to those used in most of the American lighthouses, were not Parisian but English, manufactured by the Chance Brothers who had become serious competitors.

Last keeper of the light before conversion to automation in the 1960s was the well-known Oswald Allik. He and his wife Alice enjoyed the station dwelling, which many insisted was haunted, though Alice vehemently denied a ghost lived in the attic. The dwelling is now in the National Register of Historic Places.

Heceta Head is named for Don Bruno de Heceta, the Spanish explorer and navigator who first gazed upon its green clime in 1775. Since 1894 the Heceta beacon has never failed, and at this writing the original lens still gives light, though with electrical help, not with oil lamps. (31, 38)

Newport's **Yaquina Bay Lighthouse** had the shortest active role of any similar coast facility. Now restored as a historical attraction and museum under the Lincoln County Historical Society, it is surrounded by a delightful Oregon state park. Next to the aging sentinel stands the Coast Guard lookout tower, where guardians survey the entrance to Yaquina Bay and beyond for vessels in distress.

The old lighthouse was something of a mistake. Commissioned in November, 1871, it was retired from active service in October, 1874, its first and only keeper Charles Pierce, a former Civil War captain. Demise was due in part to a geographical error: the Yaquina Head Lighthouse was mistakenly constructed a few miles north rather than at Cape Foulweather. The new lighthouse made the older frame facility obsolete. That it survived the years is remarkable. Occasionally tenants like the U.S. Lifesaving Service and the U.S. Army Engineers occupied the edifice, the latter while building Yaquina Bay's north jetty. During a long period, word rustled around the community that the building was haunted, and fuel was added to the fire when a member of a group browsing about the place disappeared and bloodstains were found nearby. (35)

Resplendent is the word to describe majestic **Yaquina Head Lighthouse.** Virtually unaltered since its inception in August, 1873, a Coast Guard inspection team recently found it in excellent condition inside and out. During its years as a manned station, keepers commonly requested that visitors remove their shoes before entering the rotunda's marble floor and climbing the winding spiral staircase leading to the top of the ninety-three-foot tower.

Located north of Newport near the community of Agate Beach, the giant tower flashes its light from a height 162 feet above the Pacific. The headland east of the lighthouse has for years been quarried to build roads. A great scar marks the location. In 1980, President Jimmy Carter signed a bill for eventual purchase of the privately owned quarry to eliminate further deterioration. Several ships have met their doom in the area and it is sometimes reported that the composition of the rocky cliffs magnetizes ships' compasses.

The lighthouse was the focal point of a recent national television production which saw it converted into a haunted structure complete with artificial cobwebs. The many moods of the lighthouse are pictured in newspapers, periodicals, and on phone book covers as well as travel folders. A radio beacon, maintained near the lighthouse, facilitates marine traffic offshore. (3, 30)

Cape Meares Light, several miles west of the city of Tillamook, stands on a bold headland 232 feet above pounding breakers. The present light, with a range of twenty-five miles, is located on a small building installed in 1963. But interest centers on the former lighthouse, now abandoned and living out its days as a historical attraction in Cape Meares State Park. Established in 1890, the squat structure contained a first order Fresnel lens lighted by a five-wick kerosene lamp. The fixture shone forth like a brilliant jewel amid a backdrop of virgin timber. Oil lamps, used until 1934, were replaced by an incandescent vapor light which, in turn, surrendered to electricity. In recent years vandals broke into the old lighthouse and badly damaged the beautiful lens.

Despite persistent rumors that the lighthouse was mistakenly built on Cape Meares instead of Cape Lookout, ten miles to the south, historical records show the site selection was made only after reports examining both capes were submitted to the 13th Lighthouse District. J. S. Polhemus wrote in an 1886 report, "Cape Meares affords nearly as good a site (as Cape Lookout) as far as the view from the sea is concerned, and being lower gives a better situation of light with reference to fog, and besides it would be much easier for construction on account of its accessibility from Tillamook Bay." Atop Cape Meares "is a flowing spring which would furnish all the water necessary for construction purposes," and, he wrote, at Cape Lookout "no fresh water was seen in the neighborhood of the point." Finally, Senate Bill S1216 stipulates an appropriation "for the purchase of a site and the construction of a first order lighthouse at Cape Meares, Tillamook Bay, Oregon."

Much of the keeper's monotonous toil was eliminated in 1934 when the lighthouse was electrified. The Coast Guard became the successor to the 13th Lighthouse District and installed an economical, automated beacon on a blockhouse a few feet away. In 1963, the stubby and stalwart lighthouse was decommissioned. (2)

Shakespeare once wrote, "Now would I give a thousand furlongs of sea for an acre of barren ground." But not all former keepers of infamous **Tillamook Rock Lighthouse** would agree. The lighthouse ranks among the most storied and fascinating of sea-washed sentinels. Commissioned in January, 1881, with principal keeper Albert Roeder in charge, the project was claimed an engineering triumph.

But for seventy-seven years the rock had a turbulent history. The victim of giant seas and howling storms which sent rocks and debris crashing through lantern panes 134 feet above the sea, the first order Fresnel was replaced in 1934 after being smashed by rock fragments torn off by cascading waves. When seas engulfed the station, the inside of the building was sometimes flooded.

During preliminary construction, an engineer who came to survey the rock was drowned, and the workers who blasted a foundation for the lighthouse were in constant danger from falling rock. The builders lived a nightmare existence on the islet. A large British sailing vessel, the *Lupatia*, narrowly missed the rock just before the lighthouse was completed and crashed on Tillamook Head with the loss of her entire crew.

Written-off by the Coast Guard in 1957, the troubled edifice has had a series of private owners who could find no proper use for the isolated basaltic upheaval. Its last owners had the interior gutted and announced the world's first sea-girt columbarium, a massive sepulcher with tiers of urns bearing the ashes of the dead. (34)

Washington

Many of the lighthouses that formerly graced the Columbia River entrance are gone, but **Warrior Rock Lighthouse,** upriver at Warrior Point on Sauvie Island (just above the town of St. Helens), maintains its vigil. In 1905 the lighthouse tender *Manzanita* was wrecked off Warrior Rock. In March, 1980 the 827-foot Panamanian tanker *Ypatia Halcoussi* grounded near the rock and tore a gaping sixty-foot hole below her waterline.

In thick fog, vessels use great caution here, often anchoring above or below the point. But in May, 1969, a runaway barge slammed into the stone foundation seriously damaging the structure. During restoration, the old fog bell was accidentally dropped into the river and cracked. One of the oldest on the coast—it saw service at Cape Disappointment in 1856, moving to Warrior Rock when the lighthouse was established in 1888-89 — the bell was raised and placed in the keeping of the Columbia County Historical Society of St. Helens.

Cape Disappointment Light Station was first recommended in 1848, but the bark *Oriole,* bringing supplies and materials for the lighthouse, was wrecked on the Columbia River bar. The structure cost $38,500 when finally completed at the 200-foot mark on a spur at the river's north portal. Illuminated in October, 1856, it stands today as a monument to maritime history.

For unknown ages, Cape Disappointment was a favorite hunting ground of the early coastal Indians, but as in most of the west, the white man took over without compensation. In 1864, Fort Canby sprang up around the lighthouse reservation, and for many years huge guns rimmed the cape, breaking lighthouse windows with their concussive blasts.

Pride of the nearby town of Ilwaco, most of the fort is now a state park. The Coast Guard maintains a major lifesaving station and training school there and continues to tend the lighthouse.

A star of hope to mariners for one and a quarter centuries, the fifty-three-foot tower cannot claim complete success, for its overlooks perhaps the largest marine graveyard on the coast. Most of the wrecks occurred before jetties tamed the river entrance. With its new paint design — white horizontal bands at the tower's top and bottom and a black band in the center, the aging sentinel defies time. (31)

Since 1898, **North Head Lighthouse** has been a companion to Cape Disappointment's beacon. It was erected because the number of shipwrecks along the North Beach (Long Beach) Peninsula, which extends a narrow sandy finger for about twenty-eight miles, had dramatically increased. Designed by C. W. Leick, a skilled, German-born engineer, built on a massive sandstone base, the sixty-five foot sentinel stands boldly at the western extreme of the point, where winds in excess of 100 miles-per-hour have been recorded. North Head is a favorite mecca of tourists, and the nearby north jetty, a desirable spot for rock fishermen. Automated like its sister lights, the lighthouse is presently on its third lighting fixture, an aero-marine beacon. Its first, a large lens and carriage, came from Cape Disappointment. For many years the companion lighthouses blinked back and forth at the Columbia River Lightship, which was established in 1892 and replaced by a huge, automated ocean buoy in 1980. (4, 51)

Willapa Bay Light, on Cape Shoalwater, glows from a sixty-four-foot skeleton tower erected in 1959. The first lighthouse to mark the north portal of the bar entrance lies under several watery fathoms. Established in October, 1858, the unique old house was undermined at its sandy foundation. Abandoned in December, 1940, it shortly toppled into the sea. Since then, the ocean has claimed acre after acre, destroying houses, buildings, farms, a lifesaving station, and sections of the highway. The skeleton tower which replaced the original masonry lighthouse also succumbed to the elements, and in 1952 was moved to higher ground.

Solution to the vexing problem, according to engineers, would be construction of jetties on either side of the Willapa bar entrance, but declining commerce probably makes this unfeasible. The question remains: Will the light have to be moved again? Coast Guard lookout surveillance of fishing craft frequenting the surrounding water is maintained from the tower.

Grays Harbor Lighthouse, near Westport, on the seaward side of Point Chehalis, is one of the Pacific Coast's tallest and an example of masterful architecture. Lifting its massive octagonal masonry 107 feet from base to lantern, this C. W. Leick-designed structure has an almost reverential personality, and well it should, for the cornerstone was laid by the Reverend J. R. Thompson of Aberdeen, Washington in 1897. Local folk affectionately refer to it as "Westport Light."

Though many shipwrecks have littered Grays Harbor, countless vessels large and small have safely used the massive tower as a daymarker and nighttime beacon. Near the lighthouse, a fog signal and radio beacon are maintained to aid the host of commercial fishing vessels and deep-sea cargo ships entering and departing. (10, 18)

Destruction Island Lighthouse graces an islet composed of thirty lonely acres, three miles off the Olympic Peninsula. The isle is surrounded by a pincushion of jagged rocks where tidal currents and slashing breakers surge in wild confusion.

Few civilians ever set foot on the sea-girt piece of real estate. Since automation, the only visitors are occasional Coast Guard maintenance crews coming by helicopter or motor lifeboat from the La Push Coast Guard Station.

Erected for the Lighthouse Service under the Army Corps of Engineers and activated in 1891, the masonry tower is ninety-four-feet high and encased in iron. You must climb the spiral staircase's 115 steps to reach the watch room, and in former times the effort was worth it, for you could see how the keepers kept the first order lens in spotless condition and the brass polished to brilliance. The light fixture has 1,176 glass prisms, including twenty-four bull's—eyes.

At Destruction, early keepers raised livestock and grew their own vegetables. And once, a bull kept on the isle knocked down all the station fences when he thought a newly installed fog signal was a rival. When emergencies arose before the advent of helicopters, it often caused hardship for the keepers and their families, as

the nearest station was twenty miles away. A derrick and hoist were used to get personnel on and off the islet, and the sea did not always cooperate when the small boats tried to land. (80)

Cape Flattery (Tatoosh Island) Lighthouse, poised at the extreme north-westerly corner of continental United States, stands void of human life. Surrounded by sea stacks and forested cliffs checking the cape's white surge, the automated lighthouse continues active and is extremely vital to navigation.

For ages, the isle was a prime summer fishing headquarters for the Makah Indians, but when the United States government decided that it was the only logical location for a beacon, the white intruders moved in without compensation, but not without difficulty. Just prior to the white invasion, a smallpox epidemic wiped out half of the tribal members. Blaming "the Bostons," the Indians became belligerent and stole tools, food, and anything else they could put their hands on. A breastwork was built for the protection of the construction crew after work got underway in the mid-1850s.

In December, 1857 the light station at the strategic turning point of the Strait of Juan de Fuca's south entrance was commissioned. At that time the population was four lighthouse keepers and two hundred and fifty Indians. Tensions between the two groups became so severe the attendants tendered their resignations, and Uncle Sam dispatched a warship as a warning to the belligerent tribesmen.

A steam fog signal was added to the station in 1871, and a government weather station was established in 1883. Landings were always difficult, and for years Indians supplied canoes to bring in food and to shift personnel. (47)

Slip Point Lighthouse, on the east side of Clallam Bay, is displayed from a white square tower on a pile structure fifty feet above water. Erected in 1951, it replaced a unique frame lighthouse established in 1905.

To gain the land when the owners refused to sell, the government instituted condemnation proceedings. Congress appropriated $12,500 for the lighthouse in 1900, but because of the area's remoteness, exorbitant costs, and lack of skilled labor, it was April, 1905 before the station was officially opened.

A standard tower was added in 1916 and the former lens-lantern was replaced by an unusual fourth order, double bull's—eye "clam shell lens." With oil-fed lamps, it was capable of producing flashes of 130,000 candlepower. Much to the dismay of those living in the nearby town of Clallam Bay, the old lighthouse was dismantled in 1951 in favor of the present automated light and fog signal.

Today **Ediz Hook Light** serves both ships and planes atop the control tower at Port Angeles Airport. In 1863, Congress set aside $5,000 to build a frame lighthouse on Ediz Hook, the narrow finger of land that encompasses Port Angeles Harbor and protects it from the waters of the Strait of Juan de Fuca. President Abraham Lincoln signed the bill to purchase the property, the edifice was completed in April, 1865, and George K. Smith was installed as principal keeper. The beacon, of the fifth order, displayed a fixed white light visible for twelve miles.

Prior to the lighthouse, townsfolk often maintained an open fire on the hook to assist mariners. The first fog signal, erected there in 1885, consisted of a A-frame bell tower with a 3,200 pound bronze bell struck mechanically every fifteen seconds.

Erosion, a constant problem at Ediz Hook, spelled the doom of the pioneer lighthouse shortly after the turn of the century. In 1908 a larger frame lighthouse on a safer acre of ground replaced it, until that lighthouse also lost ground, and in 1945 the beacon was moved to the airport where it still operates.

New Dungeness Lighthouse has shrunk with age. Built at the eastern end of a narrow, eight-mile crooked spit jutting into the Strait of Juan de Fuca, it encloses Dungeness Bay. Completed in December, 1857 the eighty-nine-foot tower showed a fixed white Fresnel light of the third order. The station's color combination attracted considerable attention: brick, its lower half painted white and its upper half painted black, it was capped by a red lantern house. Needless to say, navigators did not have trouble identifying the station during daylight, but they often claimed that it presented a strange mirage under certain atmospheric conditions.

In 1927, rumbling guns from Canadian fortifications across the strait were blamed for the deterioration of the mortar near the top of the tower. Reconstruction lowered the height to sixty-three feet for greater stability, and with the wider diameter the old lantern house was discarded in favor of a substitute from the abandoned tower at Admiralty Head.

In the nineteenth century, Indians fought pitched battles with invading tribes from the north on the sandspit near the lighthouse. The keepers, holed up inside, kept the shutters closed until hostilities ceased. In 1871, a violent gale split the spit, leaving the lighthouse on an island. Later, nature healed the breach. Today, with the increasing number of supertankers and cargo vessels frequenting the strait, the station's light, fog signal, and radio beacon have grown in importance. (17)

Today, **Smith Island Light** is displayed from a skeleton tower erected in 1957 at the center of the half−square−mile islet. It stands at the eastern end of the Strait of Juan de Fuca at a strategic turning point surrounded by kelp beds and strong currents. At low tide, a narrow traversable gravel spit connects Smith Island with tiny Minor Island, about a mile away. Through the years, the isle eroded at one end and built up at the other which forced the veteran stone and brick lighthouse, commissioned in October, 1858, to be abandoned. In recent years, that fine old structure has toppled over.

Shortly after the lighthouse was opened, a battle between white settlers of Port Townsend and Indians from northern British Columbia was narrowly averted. When several Haida invaded Smith Island, keeper John Vail grabbed his rifle and fired at them from the lighthouse gallery, wounding one in the effort.

Monarch of the historic seaport city of Port Townsend, **Point Wilson Lighthouse** flashes its red and white beams from a forty-six-foot reinforced concrete, octagonal tower attached to a fog signal building. The station, at the west entrance to Admiralty Inlet on the Puget Sound searoad, has the light, fog signal, and radio beacon essential to a passing parade of deep−sea ships, smaller commercial vessels, and pleasure craft.

The present lighthouse, constructed in 1914, was preceded by a frame structure placed in operation in December, 1879 at a time when city fathers had pegged Port Townsend Puget Sound's premier seaport. The railroads, however, which were crucial to their plans, did not share their opinion. First keeper of the light was David Littlefield, a Civil War veteran and respected member of the town. (62)

Admiralty Head Lighthouse, long abandoned as an active aid to navigation, is now popular as a tourist attraction and museum. Strategically situated on Whidbey Island, at the eastern entrance point to Admiralty Inlet, the structure was restored and opened to the public under the auspices of the Washington State Parks and Island County Historical Society.

The first lighthouse placed on Admiralty Head was established January, 1861 with William Robertson named keeper mainly because he was a Democrat. He lost his job with the next Republican administration. In those years, politics played a big part in lighthouse appointments.

In 1897, when the government decided to fortify Puget Sound and Admiralty Inlet, the lighthouse stood in the way of a planned gun emplacement at Fort Casey. In turn, a splendid masonry edifice, Leick-designed, was constructed north of the pioneer-frame sentinel.

In the early 1920s, the pattern of marine traffic began to change. Ships passed much closer to Point Wilson, and commercial sailing vessels disappeared from the scene, so Admiralty Light was deemed unnecessary. In 1927, its lantern house was moved to Dungeness Spit Lighthouse and the station dwelling became an Army officer's residence. Today, Fort Casey is also preserved under state park supervision. (57)

Marrowstone Point Light, established four miles south of Point Wilson in October, 1888, is located a short distance from Fort Flagler, now a Washington State Parks recreational area.

Due to frequent fog, the fog signal was considered more important than the light. There was one drawback, however. Navigators complained of dead spots in the shipping lanes where the bell was not audible. Despite strandings and near collisions, it was well after the turn of the century before a more efficient fog signal was introduced. In 1918, during a flurry of World War I activity, trumpets were placed on three sides of the lighthouse to warn marine traffic. (19)

Short and stubby, **Point No Point Lighthouse** resembles the land on which it stands. Located near the town of Hansville on the Kitsap Peninsula, Point No Point saw the 1855 signing of a peace treaty between Governor I. I. Stevens, representing the United States government, and one thousand of the Chimacum, Skokomish, and Clallam Indian tribes, which ended the territory's Indian wars.

First lighted in January, 1880, the station showed a fixed white light around 270 degrees of the horizon. A bell tower with a fog bell was installed nearby. In 1900 a fog signal building was attached to the tower, and the fog bell became obsolete.

First keeper of the light was John Maggs, who early in his tenure of duty was honored with an invitation to meet visiting United States President Rutherford B. Hayes at Seattle. The station log of 1882 tells of an assistant to first keeper Maggs who was derelict in his duties. Confronted by his superior, he became violent and locked himself inside the tower. The district lighthouse inspector was summoned, and when he arrived by boat a few days later, the errant assistant was immediately removed from duty and a new assistant was assigned. (32)

Mukilteo Lighthouse, immediately east of the colorful town of Mukilteo, displays its light from a thirty-foot octagonal, frame tower on Elliot Point on the east side of Possession Sound. With the ferry slip close to the lighthouse, the sentinel has a daily audience, and the ferry riders on the Mukilteo-Whidbey Island route appreciate the old building. Repeated efforts to place a modern light and fog signal elsewhere on the point have at this writing been unsuccessful. Structurally, the sentinel preserves its 1906 construction.

On the point where the lighthouse stands are the Mukilteo Treaty Grounds. There, on January 22, 1855, Governor I. I. Stevens and a number of Indian chiefs signed an agreement which ceded all lands from Pully Point northward to the whites. (59)

West Point Lighthouse, at the north entrance to Seattle's Elliott Bay, is poised on a low, sandy point. The tower is only twenty-three feet high and is attached to a fog signal building. The station, a landmark since November, 1881, remains under the shadow of deactivated Fort Lawton, which occupies the bluff east of the lighthouse. A Coast Guard attendant recently calculated that the lighthouse beacon had rendered more than 400,000 hours of nighttime service, using both oil lamps and electricity to illuminate its Fresnel lens.

Many families lived an idyllic life at the station whose sandy beaches offered summer inspiration. Countless vessels of all sizes, types, and description pass the sentinel daily. Always considered Seattle's welcoming light, the beacon is situated near the entrance to Shilshole Bay, the Lake Washington Ship Canal, and the world-famous Hiram M. Chittenden Locks at Ballard. A few years ago, an unlikely neighbor — a massive sewage treatment plant for Seattle — moved next to the lighthouse and affected its serenity. (21, 50)

Alki Point Lighthouse, at the south entrance to Seattle's Elliott Bay, stands close to the place where Queen City founders, aboard the schooner *Exact,* landed in 1851. The point was not marked by a navigational aid until 1887 when a wooden scaffold was erected and a lens-lantern hung from an arm. Hans Martin, a local resident, was paid fifteen dollars a month to keep the oil lamp burning.

With commerce increasing between Seattle and Tacoma, efforts were made to establish a lighthouse. Finally, Uncle Sam put down $9,000 in 1910 to purchase the land, but it was eight years before the present thirty-seven-foot octagonal tower and fog signal building were completed.

The station grounds are kept in excellent condition, as the commandant of the Coast Guard's 13th District, headquartered in Seattle, uses the keeper's dwelling as his residence. The original lens was replaced by a modern apparatus, and a special direction-finder calibration service was added, but otherwise the station appears much as it did in 1918, when World War I dominated the headlines. (49)

Point Robinson Lighthouse, situated at the midway point between Seattle and Tacoma at the eastern end of Maury Island, was established as a fog signal station in July, 1885. Two years later, a lens-lantern was mounted on a skeleton tower. It was not until 1915 that a first class lighthouse was constructed, and that structure, a thirty-eight-foot octagonal tower attached to a fog signal house, is still very much in use today. Former attendants considered the station one of the most comfortable and best situated in the district. There was always a waiting list for the station which featured excellent fishing, hunting, and fern-lined forest trails, as well as a steady parade of passing ships. (62)

Browns Point Light is displayed from a thirty-one-foot concrete tower at the west end of the entrance to Tacoma's Commencement Bay. A light and fog signal marked the point in 1887. In 1933, the present sentinel was erected. In 1970, a Coast Guard helicopter lifted the entire lantern assembly from the tower for repairs—an experiment which proved both timesaving and practical.

The beacon light is the guardian of Port Tacoma's sea lanes. In times past, the grounds provided a favorite picnic area for local residents. Today the station remains an outstanding place to watch the increasing number of deep-sea ships entering the busy portal.

Dofflemyer Point Light, at the east side of the entrance to Budd Inlet, on the searoad to Olympia, the state capital, is one of the southernmost sentinels on Puget Sound. The present structure was erected in 1936, but a light and fog signal have marked the point since 1887.

The early light was a post lantern. Its wick was trimmed, its bowl filled with oil nightly. This was the case with numerous navigation aids on Puget Sound before the advent of electricity. Though the light at Dofflemyer lacks the historic value of many of its counterparts, it stands proudly in a setting typical of the magnetic beauty of south Puget Sound waterways.

Turn Point Light Station, at the western extremity of Stuart Island in the San Juan archipelago, was never an impressive lighthouse to the eyes of the layman, but to the mariner its function is vital. It marks an important turning point for vessels threading through the myriad of San Juan Islands.

Turn Point was first lighted in 1893, and the present sixteen-foot concrete structure, containing an exposed light, was installed in 1936, along with a diaphragm fog signal. Scenic surroundings give the unattended station a storybook setting, free of the usual storms that often strike more exposed locations. However, swift currents and tides circle the isle.

Under the old Lighthouse Service, keeper Edward Durgan and his assistant, Peter Christianson, received a coveted letter of commendation for rescuing, in the winter of 1897, the crew of a grounded tugboat that crashed ashore.

Patos Island Lighthouse, established in 1893, was activated at the same time as the facility at Turn Point. The present lighthouse, erected in 1908, boasts a thirty-eight-foot square tower attached to a fog signal building. Located at the northwest end of the island, the light flashes its red and white warnings to vessels passing through the archipelago and traversing sea lanes near the Canadian border.

In 1905, keeper Edward Durgan and his wife moved to the station. There, they raised most of their thirteen children by filling every bit of the islet's 206 acres with crops to feed their little colony. During prohibition, rum runners without running lights made good use of the Patos beacon to smuggle bootleg liquor across the border. In more recent years, similar methods have helped ferry drugs into the United States. The fourth order Fresnel lens was removed after careless Coast Guard attendants seriously damaged the glass prisms. (25)

Located at the southeast extremity of San Juan Island, **Cattle Point Lighthouse** has an aristocratic, self-contained, concrete light tower to watchdog the south entrance to San Juan Channel. The place takes its name from the days when cattle were offloaded from the island for shipment to Victoria, British Columbia.

Erected in 1935, the octagonal tower supports a light and foghorn which is very active in the fog season between June and November. A light first marked the headland in October, 1888.

The location is historical, for it was nearby that the famous "Pig War" of 1859 almost touched off a major confrontation between England and the United States. Tensions long had festered on the island due to joint occupation by both countries. When an Englishman's pig routed the vegetable garden of an American farmer, the farmer dropped the wandering porker with a single shot, sparks flew and the respective troops of each side were brought to battle alert. Finally a treaty was signed, borders were set, and the island became American territory. (27)

Lime Kiln Lighthouse, established in 1914 and brought to its present status five years later, is an eye-catching sentinel featuring a thirty-eight-foot octagonal tower attached to a fog signal building. Perched on the slopes of San Juan Island facing Haro Strait, it is a familiar sight to deep-sea ships and purse seiners. The group-flashing light and foghorn are on the west side of the island, fifty-five feet above sea level.

Lime Kiln takes its name from the lime rock cliffs and once-productive lime kilns. Nearby Roche Harbor, now a resort, was formerly the location of the Roche Harbor Lime and Cement Company, and here, in the 1880s, John McMillan opened the island quarries and created the company town.

Lime Kiln was the last major lighthouse in the continental United States to receive electricity. Oil vapor incandescent lamps within a prismatic lens provided the light source until World War II, due to the high cost of extending an underwater cable from the mainland. (11)

Burrows Island lies in a pastoral setting, and the little frame lighthouse, nestled snugly amid a clearing with a backdrop of tall evergreens, completes the picture. Bordered by Burrows Bay and Rosario Strait on an important shipping lane, the west side of the island was graced by the tower and fog signal building in 1906. Spacious dwellings were provided for the former keepers of the light. Today, the laughter of attendants' children is missing and the once meticulously maintained grounds have gone to seed.

The island maintains its charm but is visited only occasionally by a Coast Guard maintenance crew which checks that the group-flashing light with red sector is functioning properly. Strong tide rips swish about the girth of the isle, and magnetic disturbances caused by minerals in the rock cliffs have been noted by ships passing the east shore of Burrows Bay.

The wickies or lighthouse keepers that formerly manned these sentinels of solitude may have lived an isolated and lonely life but they resided in some of the most primitive and wondrous areas of North America's coastal wilderness. Visiting our West Coast lighthouses is one of the best ways to find this coast's scenic offerings. A lighthouse is one man-made creation that can enhance, rather than detract from, the total composition of a time-crafted shore line.

Often cut off from the state highway by a broken-axle road, the rugged terrain surrounding most lighthouses is remarkably unspoiled. Today, there is growing public concern for the future of these national sites, a concern affecting the United States Coast Guard, state legislatures, and the tourist industry. The aim, finally, is to preserve these last remaining coastal watch towers, an aim I hope this collection of photographs will reinforce.

At this writing, the state has refurbished two lighthouse grounds along the California coast—Point Montara and Pigeon Point. They are leased by American Youth Hostels, Inc., as part of a growing national system. While the Coast Guard gains increased public vigilance in maintaining lighthouses, the state improves the grounds as part of its park system, and the nonprofit American Youth Hostels provide inexpensive overnight accommodations.

Another vital force in the restoration of old lighthouses, especially those now decommissioned, has been the various Historical Societies along the coast. Their active concern often turned intended rubble into permanent monuments.

There are, however, several lighthouses that should concern the Coast Guard, state and national park services, local historical societies and citizens. These include Point Conception, San Luis Obispo, Point Sur, and Lime Point, the abandoned structures at Table Bluff, and on St. George Reef. East Brother Island has been beautifully refurbished, and the empty light tower on the roof of the Fort Point Historical Site still enjoys its often visited setting beneath the Golden Gate.

The Oregon lighthouses seem to be in good hands, as do most Washington stations. Some exceptions in Washington have been Smith Island, Burrows Island, Turn Point, and Marrowstone Point. While their grounds have been in good condition, the future has held uncertainty.

The credit for getting to, and being allowed to photograph the lighthouses, is an individual story, one that I will abbreviate by extending my grateful thanks to those many park service rangers that gave understanding nods, helpful hints, off hour access, and even transportation in the San Juan Islands, and to the Coast Guard who did likewise, such as to Anacapa Island and St. George Reef. My appreciation is also offered to those individuals in the Coast Guard who shared their knowledge and time, and who were genuinely concerned with the upkeep and destiny of their lights.

I am grateful to Jim and Cherie Gibbs, whose help allowed a gallery of photographs to become printed messages, and thus shared visions. Finally, I am grateful to my grandparents who built the small cement lighthouse in the courtyard fishpond where I grew up—and planted the seed.

Chad Ehlers

All of the photographs in this book were taken with a Nikon F2 or Nikon FM body and Nikkor lenses. The only filters used were a polarized filter and an 8x neutral density filter. Kodachrome 25 was the only film used. Exposures range from 1/250th of a second to thirty minutes.

FORT POINT